The Yale Series of Younger Poets
EDITED BY ARCHIBALD MacLEISH

LOVE LETTER FROM AN IMPOSSIBLE LAND

LONDON

HUMPHREY MILFORD · OXFORD UNIVERSITY PRESS

LOVE LETTER FROM AN IMPOSSIBLE LAND

WILLIAM MEREDITH
LIEUTENANT (JG) U.S.N.R.

WITH A FOREWORD BY
ARCHIBALD MacLEISH

NEW HAVEN
YALE UNIVERSITY PRESS
1944

COPYRIGHT, 1944, BY YALE UNIVERSITY PRESS

Printed in the United States of America

All rights reserved. This book may not be reproduced, in whole or in part, in any form (except by reviewers for the public press), without written permission from the publishers.

Some of these poems first appeared in *Princeton Verse, Nassau Lit., Poetry, Nassau Herald, Decision, New Republic, Sewanee Review,* the *Nation*.

First published, April, 1944.
Second printing, July, 1944.

The Printing-Office of the Yale University Press

FOR
CHRISTIAN AND ALICE GAUSS

Now when beacons are forbidden
And from the camp
Against all dark is light outridden,
Keep you the lamp.

CONTENTS

Foreword by Archibald MacLeish	9
Myself, Rousseau, a Few Others	11
Poem	12
Who Comes upon One Standing in a Door	13
A Metaphysical Sonnet	14
Two Poems for Matthew Arnold	15
When Do We Inherit?	16
Class Poem	17
Words After Midnight, Forbidding Remorse	19
I Ask You to Consider This Great Man	20
A Girl I Knew Once	21
War Sonnet	22
After a Year	23
A Liberal	24
Sonnet	25
To the Thoughtful Reader	26
January	27
The Islands of My Desire	30
Winter Song	31
Sir, Today Is Vouched For	32
Traveling Boy	33
Quartet in F Major	34
Notes for an Elegy	35
In Strange Events	37
Love Letter from an Impossible Land	38
June: Dutch Harbor	41
A Kodiak Poem	43
Altitude: 15,000	44
In Memoriam Stratton Christensen	45
Navy Field	46
Reductio Ad Absurdum Blues	47
Airman's Virtue	48
For Air Heroes	49
Ten-day Leave	50

FOREWORD

THE foreword of this book should have been written by Stephen Benét. I think it would have been, had Stephen Benét lived. It is not ordinarily wise to guess at the choice another man would have made, whether of manuscripts of poetry or of anything else, but I know enough of Benét's likes and dislikes over twenty years of friendship to be certain that there are poems in this book he would have wished to read more than once and to remember.

I think he would have felt, too, as I do, that the later poems, the poems about the war, have an immediate relation to this time which entitles them to be heard now. They are not only poems written by a Navy flyer about the air war in an "impossible land": they are poems written from within that experience. They have an accent, a tone, of participation. They give the sense of having *seen,* of having been present, which a man's face sometimes gives, returning. They have the quality of reticence and yet of communication, almost unwilling communication, which the words of soldiers have after a difficult and dangerous campaign. And because the experience of this war, fought with new weapons in remote and unimaginable places, is an experience strange to most of us, the communication itself is unfamiliar. It has an accent of its own, an accent not heard before or recognized. The account of the experience is oblique—seen from the corner of the eye like the movement of danger at night. But the accounts of the participants in action, the first accounts, the first-hand accounts, are always oblique. Only the journalists and the historians write directly of the things that have happened, arranging them in the unnatural and artificial "order of events." No one has ever seen a war or even a battle in the "order of events" except afterward, artificially composed, like the assembled fragments of a shattered period of time, in the dispatches or the monographs.

Benét, I think, would have liked the quality of communication in the last poems of this book. He would have liked, too, the relation between the earlier poems and the later—the way in which the literary vehicle (for it is nothing else) of the Princeton undergraduate turns into the live idiom of a poet's speech reaching for poetry. Like all the rest of us, older or younger, Lieutenant Meredith has submitted to the influences. Only those who lack ears and eyes avoid them, achieving a willful and insensitive originality which, like faith without works, is usually original without producing original poems. The rest, like the poet of this book, learn from one, suffer from another, and eventually recognize the sound of their own voices over or under or through the obsessing rhythms.

The most encouraging fact about Lieutenant Meredith's work —more encouraging for the future even than the poems of the war—is the fact, demonstrated by his progress as a poet, that his instincts are sound. He seems to know, without poisoning himself in the process, which fruits are healthful and which fruits are not. With the luck of the war, which one must earnestly hope for him, there will be other and better books to follow this, but this book needs no progeny. Alone and as it is, it is work of which any young poet might well be proud—work, moreover, which is written for this time and out of it.

I think Lieutenant Meredith would like me to say by way of conclusion that we both hope, although perhaps for different reasons, that this book is the book Stephen Benét would have chosen—Meredith, because of his admiration for Benét's work as a poet and as a man; I, for that and because, more particularly, I should like this series to continue to have the quality Benét gave it during his ten years as its editor.

ARCHIBALD MacLeish

MYSELF, ROUSSEAU, A FEW OTHERS.

FROM the boy's identification
The playground difference functions,
And hesitancy here
Marks surely as tow hair
Or unnatural height from glands,
Sets the peculiar bonds.

The earliest comparing
Disclosed the need for choosing,
Where the rest played and fought;
Even the collective sport
Became only imitation
Of others' spontaneous action.

Choosing is the full-grown gland
Yet to tell it to most were unkind
(Like the off-color joke
Told to a hunchback),
Provoking a desire
For what they cannot share.

This is the daily luxury
Which alone can rouse us early
And kisses us off to work;
And to this at night
We return with promises
Until the last choice passes.

POEM.

PERHAPS some evening, following a storm,
This moon which climbs among cloud boulders
Will find itself not riding over Camelot
But close on this present suburb, relevant
To you and me and what we both must do.

But now the time is always long ago,
And the issue, if not easier, is cleaner;
And one, not yourself but like you,
Taking my face between her treacherous hands
In the manner of the last century,
Says of the lunar beauty or whatever:
"Forget, forget; all that is briefer than the fact
Is the memory of these uneasy seasons,"
And so defeats me sweetly.

WHO COMES UPON ONE STANDING IN A DOOR.

WHO comes upon one standing in a door,
    That with a sigh tries different sorrows on,
    Thinking how best to speed a lover gone,
Whether this leave or that becomes her more,
Knowing him there beside her all the while;
  Or who hears lovers worry of the dawn
  Before the white of evening quite has worn
And they not knowing dawn, and sees them smile;

Let him not presume what thing it was
  He saw enacted in a smile or sigh
  Till he pass and the door be shut and the day be high
And the lover wonders how his lover does.
  With such confused denouement the play ends
  That none but the spectator comprehends.

A METAPHYSICAL SONNET.

MORE concert than the quick have, have the dead
   Whose centripetal journeys are as one,
   While we yearn to the several quarters of the sun,
And the moon besides, and the stars, are in our heads.

And how do we follow whither we are led?
   Not like the dead, whom gravity alone
   Moves as a unit, heart and hand and tongue,
But partially, now this, now that ahead:
   Against the thing not willed, the act is done,
Against the thing undone, the words are said.

This is a stuff that cannot come to rest
   For it owns ties to heaven and to the ground;
While there are achings in the lodestone flesh
   Still will the quick move out and the dead move down.

TWO POEMS FOR MATTHEW ARNOLD

I

A CREED.

THESE were things that he found good:
    A temple ruddy with the sun,
    A scutcheon bloody with the blood
Of such and such an ancient one.

And these were things that he found ill:
    That temples should grow stiff with stone
And warriors muster so much will
    To die for truth where there was none.

II

A SONG.

I WHO love a maid despair,
    For maids are fair and earthborn things,
    With prehensile hands in place of wings;
Yet, in the spring, they sometimes wear
Roses in their hair.

A maid can sing a doleful air
With downcast eyes she sometimes sings
And be her songs but echoings,
From other worlds, of other care,
Yet she is passing fair.

So well she emulates despair,
That I who linger as she sings,
Would touch her with my sky-soiled wings
That she might walk beside me there
And people the void air.

WHEN DO WE INHERIT?

WHEN do we inherit them,
    Cromwell, Lincoln, Matthew Arnold?
    When the unengaged mind climbs and claims,
Preens old robes, and tries strange titles on
Before and after something common given;
Or reads incongruously of the projectile places?

No, but in objection shouting what they meant
Or in exertion sweating with their sweat,
No noticed intonation or gesture—
Derivative, perhaps, but in modern dress.

And even then, no real descent, no chrysalis,
But sudden brothers rather, and competitors.

CLASS POEM.

THE tale of dispensations that have passed
   Wants to be told with a nostalgic catch,
   As when we speak regretfully of Greece,
Or how grandfather dressed for dinner to the last,
Knowing that we are nowise implicated.
This is the old, becoming grief of shepherds,
This is the way men have of letting go,
Sorrowfully, of what they went to school to.
So for us here there have been days—
There have been autumn days especially,
Although the other seasons
Are hardly more to be believed—
When a sudden tree,
Or the latest Gothic trick caught in the sun,
Or just an openness that hurries in the sky,
Has been the occasion of intemperate words,
And a certain slowly cumulative passion.
(No one of course is proof against night-fondness
Which lives upon the place where the moon has shone,)
And God! how gestures made with the hand and face
Come to exact their own dependencies.
These are the things the heart remembers first,
Local, and temporal, and very dear.
None would belittle them, none would begrudge them a
   dirge.
Yet how fares the slave else when habit has come to endear,
Or how the barbarian, loving his barbarous school?
Beyond this, beyond the static affections,
There is the training for freedom we cannot disown:
We have checked over lists of heroes' deeds,
Making frugal choices; we have admired deeds

Done without honor in their times,
And drawn our solitary conclusion.
We have seen the names men call in anger
Survive to make acrostics on their fears,
And virtue, starry-eyed and unexplained,
Drawing its pay while rich men stand in queue.
In short, we are the practical ones, being sure,
While the world says: Possibly, possibly,
And: I seem to remember reading somewhere . . .
So we go out, we go out content
To be paid for service, praised for conspicuous service,
And hanged like grown-ups from a tree for crime,
Knowing where judgments come from and where they end.

Nothing is here for tears; nothing removes
Of this with seasons and tissues, and reluctance.
All is a commission and a promise
Taken among ourselves as of today.

Princeton, June, 1940.

WORDS AFTER MIDNIGHT, FORBIDDING REMORSE.

Do not say to the gay game nay now lover
    Under cover of love enough; does puritan twinge
    Predict, against respite from passion, real change?
No, we shall want again later and greatly all over.
If the angular sky was not fashioned to conform
To these warm doings, then the stars there err
For this is our way always; therefore have care
That no third sleeper come to our bed bringing harm:
Forbid Fear, whether his face be righteous as this is,
And his talk scriptural of ultimate places,
Or whether he wear rather War's unfeatured face
Who sleeps out nightly now and seduces
Many men and innocent women in their beds;
Say always to strangers that I am all your needs.

I ASK YOU TO CONSIDER THIS GREAT MAN.

I ASK you to consider this great man,
How he has known some things again and again
And how variously, under a single compulsion;
Sad seer to a day of quick ambitious cycles,
He is hopeful in the face of many never ready.
Who can say now: Ho, for the killing once more,
But said then and will say again:
Not revenge, remembering men's final requirements;
The renewal of wisdom is from action to action:
The pursuit dream becomes the dream of embrace.

With whom the great exchange their hasty necessary greetings
And even the evil share their times of possibilities,
Evil being close to greatness in its understanding;
Who unawares gives orders to the average:
It is a long time between visions for them.

Not just for knowledge or foreknowledge notice him
Or for success which is as well essential,
But stand and stare, as at a warm May day's doings,
At how nothing is the same for his fiery being,
Least of all yourself, grown active, fairer.

A GIRL I KNEW ONCE.

AS a stone city admits the brittle seasons,
    You your dependencies, and chiefly love;
    Generations from the fields, keep festivals.

A broker would not be taken for a farmer
For all he fidgets when the bushes leaf,
And I cannot ask you to lead a lover's life.

WAR SONNET.

WHOM Eros' errand sends to the ends of the earth
    I envy now, having in hand no quest;
    Buildings are bombed and walls fall in my path
Pursuing the partially-wished-for; I seem to lose interest.

Rich boys' toys which once made me sick with wishing
    Are noiseless before this bursting, the want of them broken,
And I am afraid to make friends or commence rebuilding
    With everything temporary, the very town perhaps taken.

I who have slept with sack packed, eager and dressed,
    Waiting no more warning than the morning order,
Have watched the expedition's expectations quashed
    With the coming of numberless bombers and ensuing horrors.

The maps were misplaced and most of the men dispersed,
And worst perhaps of all, I have lost the wanderlust.

AFTER A YEAR.

COLORED crucial rooms from novels fail like this,
   Windows forget their prospects, compass-spun
   With a doubtful tropism to the morning sun,
And authorities dispute where the boxwood was;

A mantle hovers between soft and strict,
Waiting for some period to be established; chairs
Shuffle uncertainly; and the speaking there,
Where each word used to sever or connect,

Is full of clauses now, no longer clear;
And with the passage of artifice and plan,
And with very great unsettlement, is seen
That never again can counsel be taken here.
   You used home solace certainty to be,
   And this way you have escaped my mind, me.

A LIBERAL.

LOVING more than another what was old,
   Still the architects' plans excited him;
   Home was razed and the culture became the man,
Loosed to assume a new and freer form.
And somehow he thought the walls would be clean as paper,
And the oaks combed like pictures and waiting,
So that coming on the completed structure
He was seized with an enormous remorse:
The native stone was bright, the lines untrue,
And the behavior of the freed men disappointing.
Committed now like the rest, around each hill
He still half hopes to come on a secret dukedom,
Old, storied, and himself the generous duke.

SONNET.

THERE was of course no saying what the end would be—
    Whether the stricken men would hold out for terror
    And the loosed machines to be caught in pits singly,
Or whether the foe would fall from happy error,
Once held to dog the steps of evil-doers;
    Or finally whether a final weariness
Might not yet unarm themselves, always surer
    Of decent private matters than of no and yes.

It was natural that his dreams should be of the victory time;
He saw himself cured at last of the old trouble
Leading a ghostly peace-pact pantomime
Or laying a city over the accusing rubble.
    But when he rose from the different dreams to go
    He would look in his comrade's face, behold the foe.

TO THE THOUGHTFUL READER.

EMPEDOCLES came coughing through the smoke
unanswered; and the Prince of Denmark's guess,
thumbing the bodkin, was substantially correct;
despondent airman plummets, but his trouble
flutters to safety like Hamlet's and the Greek's.
The sentence for destruction in the first degree:
no answer ever to the amulet question.

Add to this that all go to the grave several ways
and compose themselves elaborately as for an end
(looks back the forlornest lingerer with such longing
as forward the unsuccessful to some end-all?),
then which of us will not lie last at crossroads?

JANUARY

FOR MURIEL RUKEYSER.

NATAL month and at the year's gate,
    Known by the sure recurrent signs—
    Number and length of days, related crops,
Heats, and the cyclical desire—
Be for occasion to decking and pledging regardless,
Be ignorant of the hostile signs
Which tell no harmony with renewal:
Hazardous harvests, erratic sun-ups here.

Wisdom comes very young to these; at birth
They seem to recall what is wholly desirable; only later
Find, knowing, they are unable quite to want.
Perhaps the resolve is at nightfall, perhaps on waking,
But always the unit of purpose is a day.
They will go into the new room saying:
This and this shall not happen here.
But the body is puzzled at new restraining gestures,
Cells conserve the essential weaknesses;
And besides, they are easily distracted.
These will not be driven by derision,
Studying late with a tense hatred all friend;
Hugging knees and cursing and vowing and inward,
They will take no final revenge on scoffers,
For hatred have they none, only finding the charges inept.

Finally blessings are conferred on the little boys;
Excusing, they seek softly into childhood,
Persuasive disclaimant: "In the integrity of my heart
And the innocency of my hands have I done this thing;

Sarah you know was said to be his sister."*
But the mirror will hardly admit the evidence:
Eyes are drowsy, mouth turns down unless watched, chin is
   not good,
Only the brow is renegade responsible,
Disclosing the identity of the constant criminal.
Neither does God inform Abimelech knowing.

Time is spent projecting both extremes:
There is always the clerk's itemized livelihood,
And similarly the threat of prophecy,
But nothing named or identified in between.
Rich man, poor man, God knows what I should have been!
Perhaps I am too much admiring,
So that my muscles twitch when I watch athletes
And I am sometimes struck neuter in lovers' presence.

In between I live. Time presses me
And I have the fear that I shall be killed
By stray bullets in a holdup, curious man
Lying against the book counter, superfluous,
Or run through behind arras, listening to fighting.
In the morning to this end I tidy my effects,
Hoping somewhat to influence the judgment
When they come around afterwards;
My own I cannot influence.

Only the delights of the body
Which I am convinced are godly,
And the brave ones, do not disappoint me now.
The brave ones with black hair and good eyes
Come round like January and are sure;

*The story of Abimelech, who was prevented by God from sinning in ignorance with Abraham's wife, is used here as it is used in Genesis xx, to express the untenability of determinism.

For these only I resolve, wearing tokens
And putting checks on calendars not to forget,
Not to betray, if possible. Here, too,
The resolve is general: cleanliness, say, or industry,
And one would be foolish to wager everything on the outcome.
Nevertheless, these are the ones to think of in January,
And draw forth tricks from their trust as from a hat.

THE ISLANDS OF MY DESIRE.

THE islands of my desire
    Thrust up in a boiling bay,
    They inhabit a hostile hour
As if it were their own.

They crop when the wind is barren
    Without expense of bloom,
And when the waters anger
    Keep their wits about them.

In blight's despite and danger's
    They grow a virtuous green,
And industry is of them
    As it is not of me.

Remote and inland watcher
    Of each untoward act
I wait the weather's pleasure,
    Am not for the islands yet.

WINTER SONG.

Of course across the winter wood
   Love comes through the branches;
   Cold converts from soft to hard
And ache and chirp the birches.

But still the sky comes on and still
   The water smiles regardless
As it holds arrested in the well
   Like a rich woman, childless.

Winter love is love at sight
   With no thing carried over,
Each in the white sufficient light
   Has looked upon the other;

And who would wish the wood to Spring?
   Summer spoil the season!
Love in the winter wood has stung
   And stiffens like a poison.

SIR, TODAY IS VOUCHED FOR.

SIR, today is vouched for, and what is owing
   Will be paid, all that long borrowing;
   Let the day's portents and its tedious sad history
Prompt the guarantors to no defection;
They have professed a ghostlier dialectic
And now with first faith take up the new position.
Having made friends with the enquiring silence
And mastered all the other private torments,
They are now prepared for the complicated dragons
Which they are bound to meet. Almost pagan
Are their heartbeats and assertive voices that rejoice,
Foreknowing the day's cunning threats and choices.
Doubting as children, they were healed at a terrible spa,
And now are eager to speak for the least stammerer.

TRAVELING BOY.

HURTLED under the lover-sundering river,
    He feels at a sea-green end the journey's tension
    Between the longed-for and the doubtful place;
He is interested in the river floor above him
And in its dropped people and its sea-changed coins.
The white bellies of fish provide a weird excitement
For his concentration, and he watches squinting
The red hulls and the upward bubbling of the screws.
This dimension is comfortable, and he settles back
Beside the careless bones of a Dutch cabin boy
Whose centuries are cool and green to watch.
Riding beneath the love-dividing river,
He waits for the new commitments to be made.

QUARTET IN F MAJOR.

GREAT Beethoven, you trouble me this watchful
night
singing again again how sweet it is
this freedom, how wild it is this fight,
   singing how cunning are these enemies.

Like a white northland, icy-white and flying
   are the aspirations that scrape these chill strings,
and are not tune nor harmony nor a wild sighing,
   but strings only that hope, having known singing.

Taut strings, by whom were you taught this wisdom
   that returns on itself with such insistence
and urges love and singing for a kingdom?
   I have heard the single answer of the instruments:
Beethoven, Beethoven only among ghosts
instructs the four strings, haunts my night-strange post.

NOTES FOR AN ELEGY.

THE alternative to flying is cowardice,
   And what is said against it excuses, excuses;
   Its want was always heavy in those men's bodies
Who foresaw it in some detail; and failing that,
The rest were shown through its skyey heats and eases
In sleep, awoke uncertain whether their waking cry
Had been falling fear only, or love and falling fear.
When the sudden way was shown, its possibility
In terms of the familiar at last shown,
(How absurdly simple the principle after all!)
Any tyrant should have sensed it was controversial:
Instrument of freedom; rights, not Wrights;
Danger should never be given out publicly.
The men could easily have been disposed of,
They and their fragile vehicle. Then the sky
Would perhaps have darkened, earth shaken, nothing more.
But in practice the martyrdom has been quiet, statistical,
A fair price. This is what airmen believe.

The transition to battle was smooth from here.
Who resents one bond resents another,
And who has unshouldered earth-restraining hand
Is not likely to hear out more reasonable tyrannies.

The woods where he died were dark even at sun-up,
Oak and long-needle pine that had come together
Earlier, and waited for the event at the field's edge.
At sunset when the sky behind was gay
One had seen the lugubrious shapes of the trees,
Bronze and terrible, but had never known the reason,
Never thought they were waiting for someone in particular.
They took him at night, when they were at their darkest.

How they at last convinced him is not known:
The crafty engine would not fall for their softness,
(Oh, where were you then, six hundred cunning horses?)
In the end it had torn hungrily through the brush
To lie alone in the desired clearing. Nor the wings;
(And you, with your wide silver margin of safety?)
They were for the field, surely, where they so often
Had eased their load to ground. No, the invitation
Must have been sent to the aviator in person:
Perhaps a sly suggestion of carelessness,
A whispered invitation perhaps to death,
Death.

    He was not badly disfigured compared to some,
But even a little stream of blood where death is
Will whimper across a forest floor,
Run through that whole forest shouting, shouting.

Him now unpersoned, warm, and quite informal,
Dead as alive, raise softly sober interns;
Lift gently, God, this wholly air-borne one.
Leads out all his life to this violent wood.

Note that he had not fought one public battle,
Met any fascist with his skill, but died
As it were in bed, the waste conspicuous;
This is a costly wreck and costly to happen on:
Praise and humility sound through its siren shrieks,
And dedication follows in car.

The morning came up foolish with pink clouds
To say that God counts ours a cunning time,
Our losses part of an old secret, somehow no loss.

IN STRANGE EVENTS.

IF the moon set, and all the stars, and still no morning came, or
   If the wise few books turned changeling on the shelf, or
   If the dirty-minded enemy in such numbers came
That parleying (god forbid) seemed prudent,
Where would I then turn, oh, where would I turn then?

Men have burned hotter than stars for a lasting name, and
The books of memory are nowadays rainy-faint, and
Only the hatred of the dirty-minded enemy, only
This one face of the spinning god I always own,
(Friends can die and worse, and)
Remains white-hot and clear, so
I'd keep my very hate of this, if this or this, or
This were to come, were to come suddenly now.

LOVE LETTER FROM AN IMPOSSIBLE LAND.

COMBED by the cold seas, Bering and Pacific,
These are the exile islands of the mind.
All the charts and history you can muster
Will not make them real as the fog is real
Or crystal as a certain hour is clear
If you can wait.
            Write to me often, darling.

Thrown up hurriedly for a late-crossing people,
These are unsettled mountains where I walk,
They dance at the center still and spout new ash;
The teeming salmon remember in their courses
When they were not, and the winds run into the hills
By an old habit.

Now I am convinced there is nothing to fear,
Now on these islands you are all I want;
They shake and change and finally enchant;
But I have wished you a bawdy darling and here
Often, I, rootless and needing a quick home.

Here I have seen such singular strange visions,
So moving strong in beauty
You would not believe them, no
Not if your very lover told you so
At night remembering, stirred in my sleep at night.

One was, in the orange time of morning,
The smoking peak Shishaldin in a glory;
(Eastward I saw, oh, I remember eastward
Pavlof, the black volcano, throwing flame
At night, to seaward, when beacons were forbidden.)
Empedocles' element, neither earth nor fire;

And when I put a wing across the cone
(Snowy, and striking deeply at the memory),
It drew me, too, driven and weary
What with the war, and those foolish citizens my thoughts.

Another, the humorless mounds, the kitchen middens
Built in the painful winds that blow forever.
Watch the slow procession laying them down
(An almond-eyed people, parent to Incas and Indians)
Shell upon shell, bone upon bone, until
See they have builded there a little hill!
A thousand years, seated by this cold harbor, eating fish,
In what was to prove only a delaying action.

You are one for the day I landed there in sunshine,
Porcelain little village with your white Russian church,
Your far-eyed children and hollow-barking malemutes
That romp on the beach, cluttered with boats and flowers.
When was June gentleness set in so alien a land,
In a calendar with so few sunny saints?

A moon miracle are the milky hills at night
With streamers of snow dancing in the moon at the summits,
An ageless dance with the peculiar rhythm of zero,
And the wind creaking like a green floe.

And now I write you from such another vision.

As the haunted men who wrestle a weariness
Or women who languish from no sickness known
In books a century back, am I alone
In the sheer time of hilltop happiness.
Deft on the harbor I have put behind
The lovely gray vessels for their battles wait.
Twenty-four blue sailors anticipate

Orders of drill that drift up on the wind.
And stiff on the apron are the pretty planes
That waddle to the water and drum away,
Leaving me stammerer, inept to say
Why in their simple duty there is pain.

You will see in this passage I am wanting you.

Providence occurs to me;
I will salvage these parts of a loud land
For symbols of war its simple wraths and duties,
Against when, like the hut-two-three-four sailors
Disbanded into chaos by Fall-out,
I shall resume my several tedious parts,
In an old land with people reaching backward like many
    curtains,
Possessing a mystery beyond the mist of mountains
Ornate beyond the ritual of snow.

The moth sky of evening and the moth sea
Linger into night and coupling sleep.
Sleep for us here is a leaping down safely in silk
From the flaming bull's-eye plane of day,
Stricken ship that twists and thirsts for the metal sea.
We lie in khaki rows, no two alike,
Needing to be called by name
And saying women's names.

Now the moth descends, but when the dove?
God keep us whole and true, my distant love.

JUNE: DUTCH HARBOR.

IN June, which is still June here, but once removed
   From other Junes, chill beardless high-voiced cousin season,
   The turf slides grow to an emerald green.
There between the white-and-black of the snow and ash,
Between the weak blue of the rare sky
Or the milkwhite languid gestures of the fog,
And the all-the-time wicked terminal sea,
There, there, like patches of green neon,
See it is June with the turf slides.

Where the snow streams crease the fields darkly
The rite of flowers is observed, and because it is a new land
There is no great regard to precedent:
Violets the size of pansies, the huge anemone,
Sea-wishing lupine that totters to the brink;
Others are: wild geranium, flag, cranberry, a kind of buttercup.
In the morning sandpipers stumble on the steel mats,
Sparrows sing on the gun, faraway eagles are like eagles.
On the map it says, The Entire Aleutian Chain Is a Bird Sanctuary,
And below, Military Reservation: This Airspace To Be Flown Over
Only by Authority of the Secretary of the Navy.

Fly just above the always-griping sea
That bitches at the bitter rock the mountains throw to it,
Fly there with the permission—subject always to revoke—
Of the proper authorities,
Under the milkwhite weaving limbs of the fog,
Past the hurriedly erected monuments to you,
Past the black and past the very green.

But for your car, jeweled and appointed all for no delight,
But for the strips that scar the islands that you need,
But for your business, you could make a myth.
Though you are drawn by a thousand remarkable horses
On fat silver wings with a factor of safety of four,
And are sutured with steel below and behind and before,
And can know with your fingers the slightest unbalance of forces,
Your mission is smaller than Siegfried's, lighter than Tristan's,
And there is about it a certain undignified haste.
Even with flaps there is a safe minimum;
Below that the bottom is likely to drop out.

Some of the soldiers pressed flowers in June, indicating faith;
The one who knew all about birds spun in that month.
It is hard to keep your mind on war, with all that green.

A KODIAK POEM.

PRECIPITOUS is the shape and stance of the spruce
Pressed against the mountains in gestures of height,
Pleasing to Poussin the white and repetitious peaks.

Fonder mountains surely curl around your homeland,
Fondle the home farms with a warmer green;
Follow these hills for cold only, or for fool's gold.

Easy winds sweep lengthwise along the known places,
Essay brittle windows and are turned away;
Eskimo houses had seal-gut windows that the east wind drummed.

A fish people now, once fur hunters and fierce,
Fire-needing, they buried their dead with faggots,
And when a man went to their hell, he froze.

Remembering the lands before but much more real,
Look where aloft, you cannot say how except rarely,
The raven, rich in allusion, rides alone.

ALTITUDE: 15,000.

THE chill and stillness of the landscape here
   Edged with these rare and regular white towers,
   Reminds, oh, reminds of the faded passageway
Down which we were smuggled as children, barely saved.

Abandoned all that elegance, like this;
The houses stood, apparently quite sound,
And oh, with what an air, with what a grace,
But "Never look back," they said, "child, never look back."

One does not shout to end the quiet here
But looks at last for a passage leading out
To domesticity again and love and doubt,
Where a long cloud makes a corridor to earth.

IN MEMORIAM STRATTON CHRISTENSEN.

LAUGHING young man and fiercest against sham,
    Then you have stayed at sea, at feckless sea,
    With a single angry curiosity
Savoring fear and faith and speckled foam?
A salt end to what was sweet begun:
    Twenty-three years and your integrity
    And already a certain number touched like me
With a humor and a hardness from the sun.

Without laughter we have spent your wit
    In an unwitnessed fight at sea, perhaps not won,
    And whether wisely we shall never know;
But like Milton's friend's, to them that hear of it,
    Your death is a puzzler that will tease them on
    Reckless out on the thin, important floe.

NAVY FIELD.

LIMPED out of the hot sky a hurt plane,
    Held off, held off, whirring pretty pigeon,
    Hit then and scuttled to a crooked stop.
The stranger pilot who emerged—this was the seashore,
War came suddenly here—talked to the still mechanics
Who nodded gravely. Flak had done it, he said,
From an enemy ship attacked.
                They wheeled it with love
Into the dark hangar's mouth and tended it.
Coffee and cake for the pilot then who sat alone
In the restaurant, reading the numbered sheets
That tell about weather.
             After, toward dusk,
Mended the stranger plane went back to the sky.
His curly-headed picture, and mother's and medal's pictures
Were all we knew of him after he rose again,
Those few electric jewels against the moth and whining sky.

REDUCTIO AD ABSURDUM BLUES.

OH, the soldier he wants to be somewhere he once was,
    Or he wants to be somewhere nobody's ever been;
    The eyes of his girl shine for eight months behind his
eyes,
The unpocked lawn of home is green in his dreams.

Oh, the sailor he thinks of a roadhouse that never was,
    He remembers a strictly mythical girl called Grace
Who dances too close and knows the answers to everything;
    In his fat green wallet in dreams he sees her face.

Oh, they wanna go back to wherever it was they were
    Or they wanna go on to where they were promised they'd go,
Before the sea's sound or the shell-loud air
    Has a claim, has robbed their dreams of home.

AIRMAN'S VIRTUE.

HIGH plane for whom the winds incline,
    Who own but to your own recall,
There is a flaw in your design
    For you must fall.

High cloud whose proud and angry stuff
    Rose up in heat against earth's thrall,
The nodding law has time enough
    To wait your fall.

High sky, full of high shapes and vapors,
    Against whose vault is no thing tall,
It is written that your torch and tapers
    Headlong shall fall.

Only an outward-aching soul
    Can hold in high disdain these ties
And fixing on a farther pole
    Will sheerly rise.

FOR AIR HEROES.

I SING them spiralling in flame,
  Them gliding, all fuel spent,
  Checked by no opening silk plume:
The dedicated and the dead,
Themselves quite lost,
Articulate at last;

Sing them telling what they meant,
No small repeated dream,
As public and grandiose their want
As their last lowering scene:
Burning, dropping host,
Articulate at last;

And sing them making purchases
Beyond our furthest means,
Themselves the greatly valued pledges;
Oh, let the contract somehow be redeemed!
They speak for most,
Articulate at last.

TEN-DAY LEAVE.
FOR N.K.M. AND W.M.M.

HOUSE that holds me, household that I hold dear,
    Woman and man at the doorway, come what will
    Hospitable, more than you know I enter here,
In retreat, in laughter, in the need of your love still.

More perhaps than you fancy, fancy finds
    This room with books and answers in the walls;
I have continual reference to the lines
    I learned here early, later readings false.

More than you dream, I wake from a special dream
    To nothing but remorse for miles around,
And steady my bed at this unchanging scene
    When the changing dogs dispute a stranger town.

Oh, identity is a traveling-piece with some,
But here is what calls me, here what I call home.

THE Yale Series of Younger Poets is designed to afford a publishing medium for the work of young men and women who have not yet secured wide public recognition. It will include only verse which seems to give good promise for the future of American poetry—to the development of which it is hoped that the Series may prove a stimulus. Communications concerning manuscripts should be addressed to the Editor of The Yale Series of Younger Poets, in care of the Yale University Press, New Haven, Connecticut.

  I. THE TEMPERING. *By Howard Buck.*
  II. FORGOTTEN SHRINES. *By John Chipman Farrar.*
  III. FOUR GARDENS. *By David Osborne Hamilton.*
  IV. SPIRES AND POPLARS. *By Alfred Raymond Bellinger.*
  V. THE WHITE GOD AND OTHER POEMS. *By Thomas Caldecot Chubb.*
  VI. WHERE LILITH DANCES. *By Darl Macleod Boyle.* (Out of Print.)
  VII. WILD GEESE. *By Theodore H. Banks, Jr.*
  VIII. HORIZONS. *By Viola C. White.*
  IX. WAMPUM AND OLD GOLD. *By Hervey Allen.* (Out of Print.)
  X. THE GOLDEN DARKNESS. *By Oscar Williams.* (Out of Print.)
  XI. WHITE APRIL. *By Harold Vinal.* (Out of Print.)
  XII. DREAMS AND A SWORD. *By Medora C. Addison.*
  XIII. HIDDEN WATERS. *By Bernard Raymund.*
  XIV. ATTITUDES. *By Paul Tanaquil.*
  XV. THE LAST LUTANIST. *By Dean B. Lyman, Jr.*
  XVI. BATTLE-RETROSPECT. *By Amos Niven Wilder.*
  XVII. SILVER WANDS. *By Marion M. Boyd.*
  XVIII. MOSAICS. *By Beatrice E. Harmon.*
  XIX. UP AND DOWN. *By Elizabeth Jessup Blake.* (Out of Print.)
  XX. COACH INTO PUMPKIN. *By Dorothy E. Reid.*
  XXI. QUEST. *By Eleanor Slater.*
  XXII. HIGH PASSAGE. *By Thomas Hornsby Ferril.*
  XXIII. DARK PAVILION. *By Lindley Williams Hubbell.*
  XXIV. TWIST O' SMOKE. *By Mildred Bowers.*
  XXV. A STRANGER AND AFRAID. *By Ted Olson.*
  XXVI. THIS UNCHANGING MASK. *By Francis Claiborne Mason.*
  XXVII. HEMLOCK WALL. *By Frances M. Frost.* (Out of Print.)
  XXVIII. HALF-LIGHT AND OVERTONES. *By Henri Faust.*
  XXIX. VIRTUOSA: A BOOK IN VERSE. *By Louise Owen.*
  XXX. DARK CERTAINTY. *By Dorothy Belle Flanagan.*
  XXXI. WORN EARTH. *By Paul Engle.* (Out of Print.)
  XXXII. THE DARK HILLS UNDER. *By Shirley Barker.* (Out of Print.)
  XXXIII. PERMIT ME VOYAGE. *By James Agee.*
  XXXIV. THEORY OF FLIGHT. *By Muriel Rukeyser.*
  XXXV. THE DEER COME DOWN. *By Edward Weismiller.* (Out of Print.)
  XXXVI. THE GARDNER MIND. *By Margaret Haley.*
  XXXVII. LETTER TO A COMRADE. *By Joy Davidman.*
  XXXVIII. THE CONNECTICUT RIVER AND OTHER POEMS. *By Reuel Denney.*
  XXXIX. RETURN AGAIN, TRAVELER. *By Norman Rosten.*
  XL. THE METAPHYSICAL SWORD. *By Jeremy Ingalls.*
  XLI. FOR MY PEOPLE. *By Margaret Walker.*